I Saw You Standing
and Other Essays Celebrating Mothers

TAMARA E. BROWN

All rights reserved. No part of this publication may be reproduced or transmitted in any form or by any means, electronic or mechanical, including photocopy, recording, or any information storage and retrieval system, without permission in writing from the author.

Contact the author for bulk requests and author engagements.

~~~

Unless otherwise noted, scriptures taken from The Holy Bible, King James Version (KJV). Public domain.

Gratis use of Proverbs 31 scripture: Scripture taken from the New King James Version®. Copyright © 1982 by Thomas Nelson. Used by permission. All rights reserved.

~~~

Other creative works mentioned:
"Amazing Grace" by John Newton
"For the Good Times" by Kris Kristofferson
"Hit the Road Jack" by Percy Mayfield
"Can't Take My Eyes Off You" by Bob Crewe and Bob Gaudio
"Happy" by Pharrell Williams
"Conjunction Junction" by Bob Dorough
"Victory" by Gregory C. Curtis
"I Don't Feel Noways Tired" by Curtis Burrel
"Shake Your Tail Feathers" by Otha Hayes, Verlie Rice, and Andre Williams
Sesame Street, produced by Sesame Workshop, formerly Children's Television Workshop
School House Rock, produced by American Broadcasting Company
Little Miss Spider books by David Kirk
You Can't Take it with You by George S. Kaufman and Moss Hart.
Listening for God: A Minister's Journey through Silence and Doubt by Renita J. Weems

Photographs and images are the property of author, are used by license, or are used by written permission. See photo credits at end.

The essay "I Saw You Standing" was first presented in 2017.

Copyright © 2018 Tamara E. Brown

ISBN-13: 978-1-7326850-0-0

For My Mom, with love!

In 2017, I wrote a little essay "I Saw You Standing" to celebrate my mom's milestone birthday. I won't say which milestone (smile). I had so much fun with it that I wanted to extend the sentiment and turn it into a little keepsake, for those of us who are so traditional that we still like to have something to jot down appointments and such. And it seemed fitting to pair my thoughts of such a beautiful woman with a little trip through the traditional flowers for each month. So... this little calendar was born.

My mom has made and continues to make our days so special. I have always been awestruck by relationships of mothers and daughters. Many stories over the years of love (sometimes tough love) and laughter. That's what moms do.

If you like to garden like me, you probably agree that mothering must be a bit like cultivating flowers. A lot of what you get out is a result of the care you put in. I'll admit that most of the good things to my credit are really because of the care and diligence of a very special mom. (I'll take credit myself for the not-so-good things!) My guess is that you can same the same for your mom's influence, and I hope that this little book brings to mind many of your own special memories as you keep your days!

Enjoy the journey-
Tamara

I Saw You Standing
and Other Essays Celebrating Mothers

May

Happy Mother's Day!

Flowers are a popular gift for many occasions, including Mother's Day. In fact, the day celebrating moms accounts for about one-fourth of all flower purchases. The dianthus or carnation is closely associated with the holiday. Even so, there are LOTS of choices. But the name does make sense: Dianthus translates to "heavenly flower," quite befitting the heavenly gift of mothers.

The "Right" Mix

March winds. April showers. May flowers. Almost wherever you are (excluding the coldest of locations), May brings the thoughts of flowers—with an abundance of lovely options from which to choose.

I am a gardener, and today I picked up some plants for my patio garden. One cute pack contained a variety of individual plants, with several colors in a single pack: ruby, yellow, and orange. I selected a few packs, carefully choosing the ones that had the boldest mixture. It was an easy way to get a lot of color in my garden—without a great deal of effort. Just pick up a pack, plant, and grow.

Or <u>glow</u>, I smile wryly to myself. When the neighbors see the final floral boxes and pots: "What hard work mixing the colors." "Perfect blending them." "You really have the eye." Yes, I can hear them say it all.

"Not really," I'll reply.

"Really... <u>NOT</u> really!" I hear the voice in my ear.

I didn't need the "eye." All the hard work was already done.

Most of the time, mixing colors in a garden doesn't come that easy, though. It takes a bit of planning to get the colors and heights and textures combined in order to get the final product for which you wish. More frustrating, although there are lots of colors – sometimes too many with all the different hues—you are limited by what's available. What you see is what you get.

Except in the case of the hydrangea. It's the one flower where you can alter the color of a <u>single</u> plant. Many hydrangeas' bloom color can be tweaked.

Hydrangeas

Pick up a purple hydrangea and add aluminum (or coffee grounds) to the soil to make a more acidic environment- and your hydrangea will turn blue.

If you want the same plant to produce pinker blooms, raise the pH by adding lime. Slowly, but surely, you'll see the colors change.

Mothering must be a little like working with hydrangeas. It takes a long time and a lot of patience to get the environment right so that kids grow—and better yet, glow—ending up with some of those desirable characteristics you want in the end.

One caveat about hydrangeas: You may change the color, but the intensity is more difficult to control. It's not dial-a-shade. After all that mixing and waiting, just like the flowers in any garden or bouquet, the end result isn't meant to be "perfect." Each flower has its own uniqueness after all. However, you *can* set the direction. Maybe that's what mothers do best.

The Bible talks about setting that early direction. Using the advice given in Proverbs 22:6:

> Train up a child in the way he *or she* should go:
> and when he *or she* is old, he *or she* will not depart from it.

You may or may not be a mother—but I guarantee you've been a child. Ever thought about your journey from childhood to now? Most of us give a rare, passing thought to why we're pink, purple, or blue. We know what we are now, but we sometimes forget much of the joy and nurturing along the way that helped us really thrive into adulthood.

Somewhere along the way, someone put together the right mix. My best guess? That someone is your mom.

If we do pause and think back, we likely are flooded with memories, little stories that give color to mom's love and nurturing. Even then, we can't possibly know all of the stories that underscore a mother's care.

I imagine that was the case for one child. His mother raised him to a happy, healthy childhood. I am sure there must have been ups and downs, but I'm just as sure he felt loved by his mom.

He'd probably heard little of his mom's early life. Just imagine if he'd ever heard the story of when she almost gave him away.

Yes- gave him away. And not even in adoption to a "better" family-- Just gave him away to someone who was not in line to be "parent of the year."

Sound familiar? Yes, you know that child and the story. It's told in the third chapter of I Kings. In fact, it's one of the earliest stories we learn in Bible school. Yet, it's one I don't hear a lot and – I admit—it's one I often forget. Picture this:

> Two mothers appear before King Solomon with a fantastic tale. And a fantastic challenge for a King who wished for wisdom.
>
> Both mothers had recently given birth. While they were both sleeping, one child died. Each mother insists that the other woman exchanged the children, that the living child was her own. Both mothers claimed to be the rightful parent of the living child.

Solomon, please intervene.

King Solomon was probably happy to have asked God for wisdom. (A new chariot would not have helped at all in this situation!) He proposed a simple solution: Cut the child in half and divide between the two women.

"Fine with me," one woman said.

"Don't harm the child. Give him to her," the second woman said.

This second woman, King Solomon declared, had to be the real mother.

The real mother knew that mothering is not simply about giving birth. It's about sacrifice and responsibility. She knew that after you give birth, you give life.

Now that I have re-remembered that Bible story, I ponder the possible reason for its inclusion in the Bible—aside from demonstrating the importance of wisdom and its place in Solomon's rule.

I like to think that Solomon had lots of respect for women's roles—something we'll revisit later along this journey.

I also think there's an important illustration about the responsibility, the stewardship entrusted to uniquely mothers.

One might quickly point out that a mother's sacrifice doesn't involve whether to cut her child in half. Nonetheless, you can be sure sacrifice is involved. Time visiting the same place in the park a zillion times or reading the same book over and over and over. Sleep lost and gray hair gained. The constant quest to impart a little wisdom—to those with big mouths and much smaller ears. And, yes- loss of popularity. (Those who say "no" and make the hard calls are rarely popular at the moment.)

And, I dare say, confidence. I don't know any mother—and I know many really good, really smart ones—who doesn't think almost daily about whether she's done the "right" thing, made the "right" decision—not just for now, but for the long haul. How do you get the right mix?

As children, we just wonder "why." Why the homework and the lessons and the quotes? It's awfully hard to see how each little bit of acidity or alkalinity could possibly create the optimal environment to thrive. However, as we get older, we look back and see that each little "thing" helped to combine to make the right mix—just for you—after all. The result need not be perfection—but it worked for you.

Perhaps that's why we have Mother's Day—and why flowers have become so synonymous with its celebration: to honor all the nurturing that takes place and to honor those *nurturers* – whether they are mothers of birth or mothers of blessing (grandmothers, adopted mothers, lovingly present figures who stand in the gap).

That's reason enough to embark on a little journey—to reflect on those stories that shape our lives.

The mothers central to those stories are worthy of the honor—and whatever flowers you can find along the journey.

Your Notes & Reminders for May

Thought for May:
You may or may not be a mother—but I guarantee you've been a child.
It takes a long time and a lot of patience to get the environment right so that kids grow—
and better yet, glow—ending up with desirable characteristics.
Journey with me through the next year as we celebrate my mom and yours.
Grab your virtual vase! Along the way, before next Mother's Day:

Find (or re-find) the flower that best celebrates your mom.
Reflect on your gratitude for her nurturing.
And share that nurturing with someone else along the way.

 *May's Days*

Pictured: A flower Market

1
2
3
4
5
6
7
8
9
10
11
12
13
14
15
16
17
18
19
20
21
22
23
24
25
26
27
28
29
30
31

June

Happy Birthday to My Mom!

What four-letter word is most associated with the rose? LOVE!
The ever-popular rose is June's flower. It symbolizes humility and chastity, and the sweet fragrance brings happiness to mind.

Bunny Cakes, Banana Pudding, and Mudpies

I love to bake. I get it from my mom. When we were little, the house was always filled with freshly baked treats—brownies, sweet potato pies, and cakes.

Birthdays were especially special. The cakes were always homemade. OK... They were homemade every year except one. My mom decided to make a shortcut. A homemade cake with frosting out of the can. Many of my birthday cakes were memorable. That one especially so!

We never had frosting out of the can again! (We had a good laugh!)

My brother also caught the baking bug. (He's since lost it.) One of the things Tim and I did together (without sibling arguing) is baking apple cakes. I have lots of good memories with my big bro and making apple cakes is right among the top.

Cakes were central at other occasions for us as kids. For example, bunny cakes were the featured dessert at Easter. Every year, Ma would carefully create a bunny from two round layer cakes. One became the face. The other was carved into a bowtie and bunny ears. Add a few jelly beans and licorice for the eyes and whiskers. Top it with frosting (not out of a can!) and cover with coconut—and that bunny is ready to hop!

It makes sense: If you put something good in, you're bound to get something great out.

Our holiday table is always filled with enough tastiness to make any Southern family proud. Since I've got the baking bug, I am the architect of many creations- sweet potato pies, pound cakes, or chocolate treats. I can make most by memory. But the one thing that's never on my baking list??? Banana pudding. I've never liked it. However, I do know how to make it—or rather how NOT to make it.

My brother can chime in here: "You don't get banana pudding from mudpies." It is one of my mom's famous sayings.

When you didn't do your math homework (well): "You don't get banana pudding from mudpies."

When you didn't want to put in the little extra effort to practice that speech: "You don't get banana pudding from mudpies."

When you wondered why you needed to revise that already really good essay: "You don't get banana pudding from mudpies."

Just like hoping for the buttery best from frosting out of a can, you can't really expect genuine results from lackluster efforts.

Mom's little recipe for success is one that my brother and I carry to this day:

A lot of hard work
A little practice
Not too much procrastination
Enough willingness to change
A whole lot of faith

What goes in comes out. If you want good results, you should definitely check your ingredients.

Your Notes & Reminders for June

Thought for June:
If you put something good in, you're bound to get something great out. Birthdays are really special days- but it doesn't have to be a birthday to do something special for someone you love. It's a great day to bake something- It doesn't even matter if you use a mix (or a can) or the bakery. Just don't forget that one special ingredient: LOVE!

June's Days

Pictured: Roses

1
2
3
4
5
6
7
8
9
10
11
12
13
14
15
16
17
18
19
20
21
22
23
24
25
26
27
28
29
30

July

Independence Day

Feeling fun? The lovely larkspur is for you. Each color has its own meaning. Pink, for example, denotes fickleness.

If You Can Read, You Can Cook!

My best friend from high school and I were talking about cooking. She remarked that she couldn't cook. My mom's response: *"If you can read, you can cook."*

My friend laughed, "I can read." My mom: "Well, you can cook."

I've found that advice to be generally dependable. If I have a problem, the first thing I do is look it up. Need to make a new dish? Find the steps. Taking up a new hobby? All the background you need is in some book. Think you're sick? Look it up. (Well, maybe not- You'll definitely find something wrong- It's probably not true, but you'll find something!)

It's amazing what you think you can't do that you really CAN do—after you've read and gotten illumination. Reading is one of my favorite pastimes. When I was a child, my mom always had books around. Her favorite authors became some of my early favorites, and we still trade books to this day.

A lot has changed since I was a child. Books are now e-books. You can get hundreds of books on one little tablet computer.

It's funny (funny curious, not funny ha-ha) that despite the number of books and electronic books everywhere, many of our children don't have access to books or the opportunity to enjoy reading.

Studies by Betty Hart and Todd Risley show that children in highly resourced communities hear about 45 million words before the age of four. (Yes, 45 million!) Children from families and communities with few resources? As low as 13 million words.

A little of this gap is tied to conversations with and around children. But most of the gap is attributed to lack of reading books at an early age.

A child in a highly resourced family or community tends to have access to 13 books, while a child in a poorer environment may not have access to a single age-appropriate book, especially during the summer. Such statistics have been well documented, including in research by Susan Neuman and Donna Celano.

This is so critical because most neural connections are formed by the age of three. (And guess how I know that? Yep. I read it somewhere.... The Urban Child Institute provides lots of insight into early brain development.)

To give you a sense of how big that 30-million-word gap really is: You would need to sing all six verses of *Amazing Grace* over and over, 190,000 times!

Or, you can just start closing the gap by introducing a child to books!

On weekends, my mom and I often visited the old bookstore on Clay Street to pick up things to read. In the summer, it was the library.

Now, years later, I always try to include a book for my own Godchild. In fact, her very first gift was a big book. I sat her down on a huge *Little Miss Spider* book when she was about six months old.

Besides words themselves, books have the power to ignite imagination—taking us places far away and reminding us—just as if you can read you can cook—that you can really do anything. With them, books bring with them the sights and sounds and smells.

Yes, for me, there is a smell that I always associate with reading. It's the smell of the library in my Mississippi hometown—As I write this, I can conjure up that smell of lots of books in one place. (You'll notice a similar smell in old bookstores.) It's a pleasant smell, almost (ok- almost almost!) as pleasant as the aroma of cinnamon rolls—a yummy creation which you can learn to bake yourself by finding a recipe in some book!

Your Notes & Reminders for July

Thought for July:
Words have the power to ignite imagination. The summer is a great time to take a reading break—or better yet, visit the library or bookstore—and put a book into the hands of a child. You'll help him or her to be able to read—making it possible to cook and much, much more! That's real independence!

July's Days

Pictured: The larkspur

1
2
3
4
5
6
7
8
9
10
11
12
13
14
15
16
17
18
19
20
21
22
23
24
25
26
27
28
29
30
31

August

One easily recognizes the proud, tall gladioli. They can be depended upon to lend height and structure to arrangements. It's no wonder this long-lasting flower symbolizes strength and integrity.

There's Nothing You, Me, and the Good Lord Can't Do

My mother has a lead foot. She loves to drive—with her pedal to the metal.

She started driving early. My uncle Charles taught her to drive (a truck) when she was just a little girl. I wasn't there, of course, but I suppose he drove and she turned the wheel. And, she has been *"on the road"* driving since.

I was there when my mom got her driver's license. I'd sometimes sit in the car as she practiced in the parking lot. I couldn't have been more than seven—or prouder.

And I remember my mom buying her first car—a new blue Cutlass Supreme. My grandparents had an L-shaped driveway on their hill, and my grandad would carefully direct her "back, back, back…. You're ok," as she navigated off the hill.

It's a good thing my mom enjoyed driving, because we were certainly kids who tested her patience.

With Tim, it was back and forth to Hinds and then to Mississippi State. I enjoyed riding and seeing my big bro off to college—but if Tim forgot something, we'd go *on the road again*.

(That temporarily faded when Tim got his own car, but he ever needed something… *on the road again*.)

It was my mom who taught me how to drive. Then, she thought of a better (maybe safer!) plan, and I took driver's ed.

Then, for me, it was trips to Vandy. If I ever forgot a book, it was a little too far to bring it. But I tested patience in my own way—with lists of things I just "had" to do. Of course, I occasionally forgot that I'd left some essential thing at home, only remembering after we had gotten to the location!

If they gave a million-mile award for drivers, my mom would get the frequent driver medallion, as most moms would! From the Cutlass to a Mercury Cougar and then a Sentra and a Sable—and now a little bug, I have many memories of my mom always being there... *on the road again*.

I can hold my own on the road. When I first moved, I drove my own green bug from Mississippi to Buffalo. Of course, my mom was right there to get me settled in the snowbelt. So, *on the road again*.

Over the years, we've driven back and forth to Texas, through Florida, along the Gulf Coast. We've sung so many stanzas of "100 bottles of beer on the wall..." I can't number. And, every trip—if I could remember—has its own little funny story. (Ask her about the road to Hana!) We keep planning a trip out yonder to the West—through the desert and canyons and red rocks.

But, my most memorable car story isn't from a vacation at all. It's of my mom driving my green car.

I was in Connecticut. I had had minor surgery and arranged for a hotel room in case we needed. I was discharged the same day, but they said I couldn't drive.

My mom picked me up at the door and I thought we'd go to the hotel. But, my mother said we were driving home. Moms know that you feel much better at your own house.... So, off we were—*on the road again!*

And that's what my mother did... navigated herself onto I-84 and made her way from greater Hartford, through Waterbury (New Englanders hate that traffic-filled section on the roadway from Boston to Danbury.) She took her child safely home, lead foot and all.

It <u>was</u> much better to recoup at home. (Moms <u>do</u> know everything!)

My mom says to us, "There's nothing you and me and the Good Lord can't do."

Whenever I travel through the Hartford area, I think of that trip. I am thankful for her navigating that particular drive and for many others—both the literal ones on the highway and those along the road of life.

Unfortunately, there's no driver's ed for life's pathways. But that's okay-- when your path is ordered by the Lord. (She was right about that too!) I'm thankful for my mom, her wisdom along life's highway—and for both of her lead feet!

Your Notes & Reminders for August

Thought for August:
All is okay when your path is ordered by the Lord. Is there anywhere you'd like to go-- but have been a little hesitant? This summer might be a great time to get *on the road again*. The Good Lord will be right there with you.

August's Days

Pictured: Gladioli

1
2
3
4
5
6
7
8
9
10
11
12
13
14
15
16
17
18
19
20
21
22
23
24
25
26
27
28
29
30
31

September

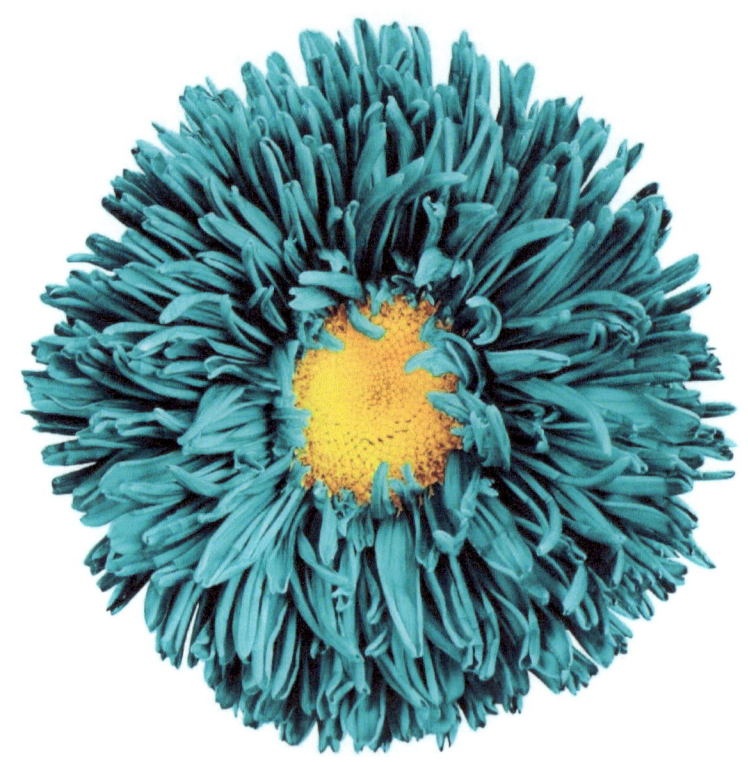

Two flowers are associated with September. The aster—so-named because of its star-like appearance—conveys love and color. The meaning for September's other choice the forget-me-not is easy to remember.

Do Your Homework and Check It Twice!

Fall makes me think of two things: the start of the school year and Christmas. (It's almost time to start Christmas shopping.) Soon, those leaves will fall, and it will be time to put together the lists of whether you've been naughty or nice—and test your recipes for the cookies you'll leave out for Santa. He is always watching.

Since we're on "naughty or nice" list making, I have a confession: I didn't do my homework.

Not this year. It was in second grade. Mrs. Johnson was a fantastic teacher who gave fantastic amounts of homework (mountainous, I recall!) So, homework became a family affair. Everyone joined in to help me get my daily homework done. I had a lot of help!

That was second grade, and it taught me one thing: (Besides the fact that families really are your best dream team!) Homework is important enough to make it a priority to get it done—and done correctly.

At home, the after-school routine was: watch a little tv, play a bit, eat a good dinner, then hunker down for homework. And just like leaving cookies for Santa on Christmas Eve, I'd leave a little something out each night before going to bed: my homework.

My mom worked the evening shift at the hospital for many years. But homework checking was always her big priority—even if it was after a long day of work. Homework was checked, comments were made, and – at 6am—homework was regifted in cases when I didn't get it quite right.

She checked. I sharpened my skills. After a while, she checked less—and I checked after myself more.

Apparently, I'm not an anomaly. There's a lot of buzz going around about what makes students achieve—things that decrease the achievement gap. I've had this very conversation about three times in the last week. It's obviously back-to-school time.

In every case, parental involvement—simple things like checking homework, asking about a child's school day, making students excited about <u>and</u> accountable for their success—were all deemed as key promoters of a love for learning and good school performance.

Even into college, knowing that someone is watching and is there to help makes all the difference.

No fancy educational theories involved—just care, participate, do what you can—and keep watching, just like you-know-who.

Now, those are really legend-worthy practices. Definitely nice.

The real monk who inspired Santa was St. Nicholas. His legend includes countless acts of selflessness, generosity, and saving and protecting children.

However, as I get ready to pen my lists, I know that we don't need Santa to recognize an extraordinary gift.

I can't tell you how many times I made a mistake and had the chance to fix it, thanks to my mom. More than the discipline of homework, knowing that you always have someone to help you get it right is perhaps the most valuable gift of all.

Your Notes & Reminders for September

Thought for September:
We don't need Santa to recognize an extraordinary gift.
It's a great time to thank some ordinary person for doing something extraordinary.
That's a gift they'll surely appreciate!

September's Days

Pictured: Forget-me-nots

1
2
3
4
5
6
7
8
9
10
11
12
13
14
15
16
17
18
19
20
21
22
23
24
25
26
27
28
29
30

October

Just a glance at this marigold and you see why October's flower symbolizes warmth and fierce devotion. Fun fact: Plant marigolds with your tomatoes to control pesky insects.

Shhh... It's a Noisy World!

When I was a baby, my family was sure I'd never talk. I'd gurgle and smile. (I guess. I really don't remember!) But, I left them all just waiting and watching for my first word.

That first word came—and as the family joke goes, the flood gates opened, and I never stopped talking!

(I probably <u>said</u> 45 million words by the age of four—I wasn't waiting to hear them!)

My mother, on the other hand, has favorite and succinct advice, inspired by Proverbs 10:19:

She that refraineth *her* lips is wise.

I say, "Let's talk." She says, "Think, then talk." Such sound advice-especially in a noisy world.

It is an increasingly noisy world. According to a report by CBS News, when I started talking in the 1970s, people were exposed to about 500 advertisements per day. Now, estimates indicate that we see nine or ten times as many ads—almost five thousand ads every day, telling us what to buy or what to wear, trying to influence what we do and how we think.

I tested this today while I watched TV, checked email, and scrolled through those annoying phone ads that won't let you finish reading content on your phone:

A TV commercial promises to get rid of all of my credit card debt. (Note: It "only" takes the equity in my home to erase all the debt away. And then, I can live the life I was meant to live. In other words, I can buy, buy, buy more, more more.)

A new product promises to get rid of my wrinkles. (Translation: It's okay to get older—just don't look older.)

A pop-up promises to provide the list of "must-buy" stocks. (I admit. I did click on that one. The catch is, I'll have to pay $19.99 per month to get the list.)

These messages are constantly vying for our time, our money, our behaviors, and our thoughts.

Who really determines the life you want to live, how you define beauty, what you value?

With all the noise, sometimes you feel the need to shout, if only to make sure you have your own attention.

The good thing is, we don't need to vie for attention amidst all the noise. We already have everything we need: the power of our own convictions. Think. Then talk. (Or spend, or buy, or dress. Or, vote.)

If you are rooted in the things in which you believe, all the noise is just... nonsense!

You can refrain your lips, but you don't ever refrain your sense of your own convictions.

Good advice—especially in a noisy world.

Your Notes & Reminders for October

Thought for October:
We already have everything we need: the power of our own convictions!
This month's thought is appropriately short, in honor of brevity!
But- it comes with a big opportunity to do one of my favorite things (talk!): Find one thing in which you really believe—and share it with someone in the next generation. It'll help him or her to navigate the noise and find the power of personal convictions!

October's Days

Pictured: Marigolds

1
2
3
4
5
6
7
8
9
10
11
12
13
14
15
16
17
18
19
20
21
22
23
24
25
26
27
28
29
30
31

November

There are many varieties of mums. Some people believe they bring joy and friendliness into a home. Looking at one of Tamara's favorites, the neon spider mum, certainly inspires a bit of cheer. The lovely peony is also associated with November. It symbolizes abundance and is another of Tamara's favorites. You'll see one of her own peonies next May.

What Big Eyes We Have

It's November. My birthday month. I'm getting older, but like all children, I'm compiling my birthday wish list. The more things change, the more they stay the same. This brings me to thoughts of many wishes before.

It wasn't for a birthday, but I distinctly remember one thing that I REALLY wanted as a child: a Pez. You know that now-retro candy dispenser with the little colored candies in the fun colors. My mom and I were in K&B Drug Store. Of course, at the register, was a Pez. I grabbed it. Just like the wolf in the fairy tale, what big eyes we have!

My mom gave a firm "no." I begged for it, cried and cried. So, I did get something: A lecture that you don't need everything you see—and to stop acting up in public.

All my crying was to no avail. Until—a man behind us bought it and handed over to me.

I was happy.

Momentarily.

Until I got a second lecture that "no" really meant "no"—and you can't whine about everything you don't get.

That took all the fun out of the Pez.

I learned the lesson. So well, that I later recall wanting to go somewhere (for ice cream or something) and was told "no."

I didn't whine. My mom was so pleased that I didn't whine; she took me for ice cream later and complimented me for behaving with some degree of maturity.

I got the message.

I'm not sure if there were fruity flavors in that Pez, but the Bible does talk about the importance of developing maturity in the areas of a few "fruits." There are nine such fruits of the spirit:

> But the fruit of the Spirit is
> love, joy, peace,
> longsuffering, gentleness, goodness,
> faith, meekness, temperance:
> against such there is no law.
> Galatians 5:22-23

Note two of these: longsuffering and temperance. My translation: patience and self-control.

Along with contentment, those are ultimately my lessons from the fateful Pez.

I've found that life is full of stuff on display. We all want to enjoy life, and there's so much from which to choose!

Contentment, patience, and self-discipline aren't signs of weakness or lack of ambition.   (It <u>was</u> the wolf with the big eyes, after all!)

Just maybe—It's more important to first enjoy what you have so you can later have what you enjoy.

My wish list doesn't need to have everything I see—unless it's a little more fruit!

As I approach this birthday, that's a real sign of maturity!

Your Notes & Reminders for November

Thought for November:
The Bible does talk about the importance of developing maturity in the areas of a few "fruits." I find some of them hard to practice, but we have to keep trying.
(A couple of years ago, I was in CVS. A little boy at the counter was crying and crying over some candy that he wanted, and his father wouldn't budge. Yes- I bought it for him!)
Oh, well...kindness is also a "fruit!" Find your own favorite "fruit" to practice this month.

November's Days

Pictured: A spider mum

1
2
3
4
5
6
7
8
9
10
11
12
13
14
15
16
17
18
19
20
21
22
23
24
25
26
27
28
29
30

December
Merry Christmas!

Want to wish someone good cheer? Well that's the mission of the poinsettia.
Sharing December with holly, this plant is a popular gift to share at Christmastime.

Entertaining Angels

We love Columbo. You know, the friendly detective who is absolutely annoying and deceptively clever. His famous line asking for *yet another thing* and his tattered overcoat are legendary.

In one episode, a kind nun mistook him for a homeless person. When he told her he was a detective, she was even more sorry that he was in such a state with full employment.

His roundabout nonsense, clumsiness, and disheveled appearance inspires you to do one thing. Turn. Then, look the other way and run!

We've all run into Columbos in our lives.

I certainly have. My mother jokes with me that there's some sort of "Open for Talking" sign that hovers over me. Once, as we were shopping for holiday dinner, I was stopped by a woman who wanted to know what herbs I was picking for my turkey. She always stuffed an apple in her turkey; I fill the turkey with rosemary, thyme, sage. She decided to add those to her apple, and as we gave each other a happy send-off, my mother remarked that I apparently had had a good conversation with my friend.

Good conversation, yes. Friend, not exactly. I didn't know her at all.

I once ran into an elderly woman who heard me talking and declared I must have been a hillbilly. Just how did she know? She was a hillbilly too. And to prove it, she started singing a country song. Yes, I have met many Columbos.

Columbo reminds me of the Biblical Anna and Simeon—two people hanging around the temple, waiting for something, expecting a solution to a puzzle everyone else doesn't know exists. In today's day, they would be labeled a little odd. (Maybe they were labeled odd then as well.)

One day, Simeon and Anna finally found the very person for whom they had been waiting. In walk Mary and Joseph with a little baby named Jesus.

Ha! Anna and Simeon really did know something after all!

Simeon walks right up and takes the baby in his arms. Anna walks in and starts prophesizing about the redemption of Jerusalem. (It's in the second chapter of Luke. Really, women have been central to the church for a very long time! Just thought I'd throw that in!)

My mom loves poetry, and so we as kids got a lot of it, the way some kids are spooned cod liver oil. One favorite from Edgar Guest:

> I have to live with myself and so
> I have to be fit for myself to know
> I have to be able as days go by
> Always to look myself straight in the eye.

I can remember most of the lines to this day. What I really remember, however, is the meaning: At the end of the day, you have to do the right thing. At the top of the "right thing" list?

Treat other people with respect.... Don't judge people by what they have.... Do unto others....

It's never a bad time to give a welcoming smile and to take the time to really <u>see</u> the person in front of you.

At worst, you have extended to another the kindness that all of us as children of God deserve. Every once in a while, your pausing might just make someone else's day a little lighter.

At best, like in the case of Simeon and Anna, you have entertained angels.

Be not forgetful to entertain strangers:
for thereby some have entertained angels unawares.
Hebrews 13:2

Your Notes & Reminders for December

Thought for December:
It's never a bad time to give a welcoming smile and to take the time to really <u>see</u> the person in front of you. This Christmas season, say, "hi" if you see Columbo.
He or she might just be an angel.
(Or, you might get the chance to be!)

December's Days

Pictured: A poinsettia

1
2
3
4
5
6
7
8
9
10
11
12
13
14
15
16
17
18
19
20
21
22
23
24
25
26
27
28
29
30
31

January

Happy New Year!

Need a hardy flower? Look no further than the carnation. Symbolizing distinction, this flower is a go-to for occasions like Mother's Day, weddings, and award ceremonies.

Pass It On

If you didn't have enough calories in Thanksgiving and Christmas, you can always catch up in January.

The New Year's Day meal for most Mississippians is one steeped in tradition—and it was one that I happily carried with me to Western New York.

One of the best things about New Year's dinner is that it's really the simplest of foods, combined with its own little formula. You may have grown up passing around a similar set of dishes at your mom's table:

> Black-eyed peas for good luck
> Some greens for money
> A little pork- a sign of prosperity
> Cornbread for gold
> And sweet potato (not sure why, but why not???)

We always have meat or poultry. Some people believe that chickens aren't the luckiest of creatures. But really, how lucky would a dinner be without the bird—or some substantial protein?

Growing up, I wasn't a fan of black-eyed peas. Yet, my mom always gave me a spoonful—just to set up good luck for the year.

I suppose that I could have stopped eating them as an adult—but if you come to my New Year's Day dinner, there they are! It's a tradition after all. If you've ever had my black-eyed peas, they are a little different from my mom's. Mine are a lot drier, St. Lucia style.

And that's okay. In her book *Listening for God*, my former professor Reverend Dr. Renita J. Weems tells a story about an ancient community who had a traditional way of calling God. (It's been years since I read the book; I hope I recall the substance of the story!)

The community gathered together in a specific place. They sang a specific song, danced a specific dance, and said a specific prayer. At the end, God's spirit always appeared.

That tradition was passed along from generation to generation. Many years later, the descendants didn't know the exact place. They hadn't learned all the verses of the song. Nor could they say such an eloquent prayer. They could dance, but they didn't know the traditional steps. In fact, all they did remember was that it was important to get together and to call on God.

So- they did. They got together, sang a song, danced and prayed the words of their heart. It looked totally different than from their ancestors' time.

But guess what? God's spirit appeared.

Somewhere along the years, the ancestors may have lost all the little nuances in the instructions, but they never failed to pass along what was truly important.

(Interesting side note that perhaps most aptly proves the point: As I was finishing this book, I searched for Dr. Weem's account to see *just how good* my memory of this story was. You'll have to read it for yourself to see if you agree that the gist is the same. However, there are a few distinct differences from my attempt to retell the tale. Her story recounts a Jewish legend of Baal Shem Tov. Yes, there *was* a special place and a prayer, but no special dance. There also was the lighting of a fire, something I'd completely forgotten. In the end, she relays that God appeared; so, I guess I remembered the most important thing about the story after all.)

When my mom looks at her New Year's table now, it surely bears a striking (but probably not exact) resemblance to the one from her childhood—my Granny's table. She was a woman who believed in family. "You always remember your family" was her advice.

In his second letter to Timothy, Paul remarked on the young man's "unfeigned" faith—one that was passed along from (where else, of course?) his mother Eunice and grandmother Lois. Paul's own "cooking" advice in light of that faith:

>...stir up the gift of God....
>from II Timothy 1: 5-6

More important than food traditions, family pass along faith—sometimes in the most meandering ways.

Food. Family. Faith. What a great combination to pass around your New Year's table.

Your Notes & Reminders for January

Thought for January:
"Stir up the gift of God." January is a great time to start the year off right.
Call your family, cook some food, and invite God in!
It really doesn't matter about the details. You'll be sure to set up a fabulous New Year,
where you can fully use the gifts God has passed along to you.

January's Days

Pictured: Carnations

1
2
3
4
5
6
7
8
9
10
11
12
13
14
15
16
17
18
19
20
21
22
23
24
25
26
27
28
29
30
31

February

Happy Valentine's Day!

F is for faithfulness.... That's a clue for February. You have your choice of official flowers for February, the violet and the iris. They symbolize not only faithfulness, but wisdom and hope, which are nice thoughts during the cold winter!

That's My Song!

Most people have a song that was the soundtrack for a portion of your life.

Since Valentine's Day is approaching, the song playing in your head may just be about someone you love.

Perhaps you loved Al Green's "For the Good Times." For others, maybe it's "Hit the Road, Jack." I hope it might be "Can't Take My Eyes Off of You."

Or, maybe you're just "Happy." (I find myself clapping every time I hear that song!)

I'm a *Sesame Street - Schoolhouse Rock* kid, so I grew up on "Conjunction Junction." That's the weird song that came to mind when I first started this month's note.

Truthfully, it would be more appropriate to have had another song in my head. About the place where I am now. A whole country, in fact: *Procrasti-nation.*

It's one of my favorite places. (Must be, since I visit so often!) I've visited several times in the last week, as I've been finishing up this little book.

My mother has a favorite saying. You've probably heard it many times:

> If a job is once begun, never leave it until it's done.
> Be the labor great or small—
> Do it well or not at all.
> -Origin unknown

Such fine words—and ones she always puts to practice.

I first knew that when I was in first grade or so—certainly before I even knew the word procrastination.

My mom graduated nursing school and when I saw her graduation picture in the newspaper, I knew she had finished something wonderful. I wanted to be a "finisher" too.

I still have that graduation picture. It still engenders proud memories.

When I talk to students about success—especially girls about pursuing their dreams—I tell them that two things are essential: hard work and finishing what you start. The world needs people who can be counted on to be finishers. That's a value I learned, first, from my mom.

Over the years, that pattern held true. My mom always finishes—and she believes in doing things well.

...or not at all! ☺

So, at least for today, I'm turning off *Procrastination* and playing a new song.

Perhaps "Victory." Or, "I Don't Feel Noways Tired."

Or—just maybe—"Shake Your Tail Feathers!"

Your Notes & Reminders for February

Thought for February:
If a job is once begun, never leave it until it's done.
Now that January is over, it's time to make some real resolutions.
Ready to sing a new song? February is a great time to set a goal for the year
—and keep working until it's finished.

February's Days

Pictured: Deep Purple Iris

1
2
3
4
5
6
7
8
9
10
11
12
13
14
15
16
17
18
19
20
21
22
23
24
25
26
27
28
29 *(if a LEAP Year!)*

March

Also known as the jonquil, daffodil blooms are among the finest signs of spring and represent rebirth.

The Little Things

Turn on the television. Chances are you'll see a show about people in tiny houses. Not small houses. Teeny-tiny houses. Typically ranging from 100 to 200 square feet, they are part of a movement to discourage wastefulness and promote decrease.

Now, I actually like the concept of decrease—but I think tiny houses are a bit much! (Excuse the pun.) The only way I could live comfortably in a tiny house would be to build it on a large lot—and then camp in the backyard. A tiny house might be okay if you can spend lots of time outdoors.

Spring arrives this month and with it the chance to enjoy those outdoors. Psalm 24:1 reminds us that "the Earth is the Lord's." There are so many wide beautiful spaces in God's creation to enjoy.

Growing up, we spent lots of time in those big open spaces. Trips through the National Military Park. (I must have read every state's monument 50 times!) Beaches from Biloxi to Hawaii. And our own yard.

My mom had yearly Easter egg hunts at home for me and just a few friends. Sometimes we'd just grab ice cream and some quick food to picnic in the park. I remember building sand houses on the beach.

Over the years, we've been blessed to enjoy some really cool vacations. A lot of big experiences, I suppose. But however big they may have been, they could never remain memorable without the people and special nuances.

I loved the Musée d'Orsay in Paris. That's certainly a big place with big art. I have such fond memories of Paris and particularly that museum. But, really, what <u>first</u> comes to mind about when I hear the name is how my mom and I laughed running back to our hotel—certain we were being chased by one of Paris' famous *les rats*. (In that case, we really hoped it was a little thing!) Just so I don't leave a prevailing image of Paris rodents, I also fondly recall another favorite "little thing" from Paris: delicious chocolates. Well worth the trip.

Hmmmm- For such big spaces, I have big memories—but they are really of such little things. Tiny things. Like happy moments and good friends. Tasty ice cream. Laughter.

Isn't that the way it should be?

Jesus found himself at a <u>big</u> party with two of his favorite people, the sisters Mary and Martha.

Martha—and I can sympathize with her—was focused, exasperated even, over preparations for the big event. I've been Martha. There are invitations and flowers and colors and guest lists and food and allergies—and timing. Because what use is there in having an event, if everything happens at the wrong time.

Meanwhile, Mary just wanted to enjoy the moment with Jesus. Mary wasn't focused on the huge event. What was the use in having the perfect event, if you missed enjoying the people who were there?

Mary was focused on what Jesus called, "that good part." (Luke 10:42)

Kind of flip-flops what's big with what's important, doesn't it? Just maybe those tiny-house-people know a thing or two after all!

Your Notes & Reminders for March

Thought for March:
"The Earth is the Lord's."
Spring really is springing. If you look closely, little signs of growth are everywhere.
Take time to enjoy the daffodils—and all the little things that make life grand!

 ## March's Days

Pictured: Daffodils

1
2
3
4
5
6
7
8
9
10
11
12
13
14
15
16
17
18
19
20
21
22
23
24
25
26
27
28
29
30
31

April

Choose daisies or sweet peas for April. The daisy, pictured above, is the flower of innocence. Sweet peas symbolize goodbye—but don't let that make you sad. Traditionally, sweet peas are flowers to convey gratefulness; so, they make a great gift after enjoying dinner at someone's home.

The Ides of April

My mother always reminds me when it's tax time. The Ides of April. It's the time when we pull together a lot of stuff about which we haven't given a great deal of thought over the last year.

Actually, that's not really true. We probably spend significant time thinking about taxes: How much they are. How unfair they are. How do I get them to be smaller and smaller? (About last month's concept of decrease: <u>Everyone</u> loves decrease when it comes to paying taxes.)

I was recently talking to someone about "grossing up." Sounds unpleasant, but that's not true, either. (That's my second untruth so far this month.) Grossing up is actually fantastic. It's when someone pays you more to compensate for the taxes that will eventually come out. Pity it doesn't happen very often! If everything was "grossed up," taxes would be fun.

I happily started my first part-time job when I was about sixteen. I was sure then that one nice thing about taxes was that they would eventually go away. At some point, I surmised, you must get too old to pay taxes! (As I am now "older," I know that that's definitely not true.)

If it's not income tax, it's social security tax or property tax or sales tax! You grow up only to find you'll spend even more and more time – looking at lists of *the best states to retire*. (By the way, those lists are not aptly named. Perhaps they should be called *the best states to reduce your taxes*. Happy taxes, happy retirement, I suppose.)

I can only recall one time when taxes were a fun topic. My mom and I saw the play *You Can't Take It with You* a few years ago—with Grandpa played by James Earl Jones, a man who can deliver the funniest lines with a straight face.

There's a line in the play where Grandpa is arguing with the tax man, who insists that paying for government, congress, and the president must be reasonable things to fund from citizens' taxes. Grandpa considers this and agrees with the principle—just not with his money.

The premise of the play is that you can spend all your life focused on money, having money, keeping money—but you can't take it with you. Novel concept.

Sorry- that's not true either. The concept is true, but it's not novel. The original movie *You Can't Take It with You* premiered in 1938, I believe- but the concept is really much, much older:

Jesus is sitting on a mountain and starts a sermon, one focused on grossing up on all the right things in life. Somewhere in that sermon, He admonishes us to forget accumulating stuff that is temporary and easily lost.

Focus, He says, on that which is everlasting...

>For where your treasure is, there will your heart be also.
>Matthew 6:21

My mom is right: It is time to file taxes.

Then, go off and spend the rest of the year doing something really important: watch a play (or tv) with someone you love—or do something else you enjoy. Whatever it is, let's amass an entirely different type of treasure.

Your Notes & Reminders for April

Thought for April:
April not only contains Tax Day; the month starts with April Fool's Day—hence the number of things that were *just not true* this month, including the very start of the note. One last fun fact: April 15 is <u>not</u> the Ides of April. (Yes, March 15 is the Ides of March!) However, April's Ides is probably the 13th. That really doesn't matter—and neither does much of what we spend so much time thinking about. So, pay your taxes… then, have some fun doing some real treasure building!

April's Days

Pictured: Sweet Peas

1
2
3
4
5
6
7
8
9
10
11
12
13
14
15
16
17
18
19
20
21
22
23
24
25
26
27
28
29
30

May

Happy Mother's Day!

Although the "official" flower of Mother's Day is the carnation, the flower for May is the lily of the valley, which symbolizes appreciation.

I Saw You Standing!

Mother's Day is a day for flowers. In fact, it has an official flower: the carnation.

I have never been a huge fan of carnations, I'll admit. Luckily, there are many choices for Mother's Day. You know them: pink or white orchids, lovely stargazer lilies, lovely pale roses, lovely lilies of the valley.... And my own favorite—peonies!

Peonies from Tamara's garden in Buffalo

Now, peonies absolutely fit the bill when your thoughts turn to Mother's Day. They are pale and pretty. So spectacular that you wait and wait and wait for their arrival—and then you enjoy the fresh sweet fragrance—something for which ants will march miles—hoping against hope that the rain doesn't come too soon against those precious petals. So beautiful. So sweet. So fragile. Just like mothers.

Like mothers???

No. Actually, not like mothers at all!

I've come to believe that we've all been the subject of a big *flim-flam*. Just take a look at Proverbs 31, the Biblical passage of the ideal woman/wife/mother. (Yes, we've made it back, full circle, to Solomon.)

>She is smart.
>*She opens her mouth with wisdom.*
>
>She is resourceful.
>*She makes linen garments and sells them.*
>
>She is busy.
>*She also rises while it is yet night and provides food to her household.*
>
>She is proactive.
>*She considers a field and buys it; from her profits, she plants a vineyard.*
>
>She is helpful.
>*She extends her hand to the poor, Yes, she reaches out her hand for the needy.*
>
>Excerpted, Proverbs 31: 26, 24, 15, 16, 20 (NKJV)

She's not waiting or at another's whim. She's not idle. Neither is she confused nor is she dim-witted.

She's neither a passive carnation or a sit-on-the-shelf rose. She's not there just to gather lily admiration.

And (I'll even admit!) she's not a fragile peony afraid of a little rain.

I'm not sure why we persist in these perceptions of light, fluffy women—when the reality is so, so much better!

The woman in Proverbs 31 is a prize. And if there's a fitting flower to honor her, it's the *adenium obesum* or the desert rose. It's a beautiful flower, usually a vibrant pink much like an azalea. It isn't a rose at all. It's actually a succulent (in a family of plants similar to cacti, in the sense that it, like the proactive woman in Proverbs, holds on to water—just in case it needs it later).

The rock or "desert" rose

That vibrant pink flower is accompanied by evergreen leaves. The combination is a beautiful, strong, hearty flower.

And that mother? She's a survivor. She can handle the drought. She's smart, and she makes her way for herself and her family.

The Bible starts off calling her "virtuous," and we often stop there. But the Proverbial writer—perhaps the wise Solomon—goes much further. And, I agree with that writer. Me? I call her the smart, resourceful, helpful, proactive, busy woman!

And if you know her, you know my mom. (I'll bet this describes a mom in your life too!)

It takes strength to make the decision to divorce and raise children alone. It's not easy to learn how to drive (and buy a car ta-boot!), to go to college, or to earn your nursing license. Neither is it a walk in the park to work hours to put your children through the schools of their choosing. It's not easy to be there whenever your parents or kids—even your grown kids—need. And to be that constant source of love and advocacy for your family.

It wouldn't be easy to do one of those things. It's "darn tootin" not easy to do them all. But my mother did—and she still does.

Gracefully. (And that's not easy either!)

I have a prevailing picture of my mom in my head. It's from my undergraduate graduation. As I walked across the stage, she stood and she yelled, "Yaaaaay, Tara."

The funny thing is that I didn't hear her over the crowd. In fact, I didn't see her either, with so many people. But we laughed about it later.

But, I can definitely feel her pride from that day. And, in my mind's eye, I can "see" her standing there.

And how am I so sure of that picture in my mind? It's simple. Because, I _have_ seen her standing many, many times.

Standing up to make a better life for us. Standing up while checking homework. Standing up to buy a car or a house. Standing up caring for my grandparents. Standing at the hospital. Standing up for me and my brother.

And because she has always stood for us, we stand now.

I've seen her standing hundreds of times in my life.

I doubt if she's ever even noticed me watching—she's been so busy—

—but, Ma'am, I saw you standing!

Your Notes & Reminders for May

Thought for May:
The Bible starts off calling her "virtuous," and we often stop there. But the Proverbial writer—perhaps the wise Solomon—goes much further. And, I agree with that writer. Me? I call her the smart, resourceful, helpful, proactive, busy woman!
May is a great time to celebrate <u>all</u> those women who are truly rock roses!

# May's Days

Pictured: The rock or "desert" rose

1
2
3
4
5
6
7
8
9
10
11
12
13
14
15
16
17
18
19
20
21
22
23
24
25
26
27
28
29
30
31

Photo Credits

Inside book, in order of appearance
Vintage flowers collage: Vera Petruk, *I Stock Photos* by Getty Images
Flower market: Zbynek Jirousek, *I Stock Photos* by Getty Images
Hydrangea: Linjerry, *I Stock Photos* by Getty Images
Rose: Studio Porto Sabbia, *I Stock Photos* by Getty Images
Larkspur: Oleksandr Kostiuchenko, *I Stock Photos* by Getty Images (also on cover)
Gladiola: Lola Lar, *I Stock Photos* by Getty Images (also on cover)
Gladiola: Olga Niekrasovo, *I Stock Photos* by Getty Images
Aster: Boxer X, *I Stock Photos* by Getty Images (also on cover)
Forget-me-not: Victoriya89, *I Stock Photos* by Getty Images
Marigold: David S. Mohn, *I Stock Photos* by Getty Images
Marigold: UseraSd5a372_15, *I Stock Photos* by Getty Images
Chrysanthemum: Tamara Kulikova, *I Stock Photos* by Getty Images (also on cover)
Poinsettia: Irina Drazowa-Fischer, *I Stock Photos* by Getty Images
Poinsettia: Irina Drazowa-Fischer, *I Stock Photos* by Getty Images
Carnation: y-Studio, *I Stock Photos* by Getty Images (also on cover)
African violet: Aadisa, *I Stock Photos* by Getty Images (also on cover)
Iris: Barilo Irina, *I Stock Photos* by Getty Images
Daffodil: Elena Kratovich, *I Stock Photos* by Getty Images (also on cover)
Daisy: Elena Volkova, *I Stock Photos* by Getty Images
Sweet peas: T. OTSUKA, *I Stock Photos* by Getty Images (also on cover)
Lily of the valley: Anna-Mari West, *I Stock Photos* by Getty Images
Peony: Tamara Brown
Rock rose: Joejoesang, *I Stock Photos* by Getty Images (also on cover)

Front cover only, not appearing inside book
Gladiola (*first row, third picture*): Olga Niekrasovo, *I Stock Photos* by Getty Images
Marigold (*second row, second picture*): The_interpro, *I Stock Photos* by Getty Images
Poinsettia (*third row, first picture*): WDnet, *I Stock Photos* by Getty Images

Monthly "Thought" Pages
Borders: neyro2008, *I Stock Photos* by Getty Images

Back Pages, Back Cover
Author photo: Douglas Levere, SUNY Buffalo
Pink roses, from author's garden: Tamara Brown

Tamara E. Brown loves seeing things grow—whether a medical device, chemical plant build, future careers for children in STEM, or (of course) things in the garden! (NB: She is pictured in one of her gardens in Buffalo.)

Named a White House Champion of Change in 2011 and one of *Fortune* Magazine's Heroes of the 500, her work experiences have informed her personal passion: creating opportunities so that others can realize the potential in their lives. In the last fourteen years the *Tech Savvy* program she founded has introduced thousands of middle school girls across the country and the adults in their lives to the multiple possibilities in science.

Tamara earned her undergraduate degree from Vanderbilt, double-majoring in biomedical engineering and chemical engineering, a master's degree in chemical engineering from the University at Buffalo, and an MBA from Canisius College. A lifelong learner, she recently completed a Harvard Business School program in sustainable business strategy.

Her career has spanned the fields of medical device development, technology project management, sustainable development and community engagement.

She calls Mississippi home and enjoys living and working in Western Connecticut, where she also writes and gardens, but neither frequently enough!

Always careful to emphasize that what you do doesn't completely define who you are, she is most importantly: a child of God, friend, niece, cousin, sister, and honorary lifelong Western New Yorker. She is Godmother to undeniably the most astute young lady in the universe-- and, of course, she is a daughter!

Connect with Tamara by email: letsconnect@stemfabulous.org